Great Railway Eras

ISLE OF WIGHT LINES
50 years of change

Vic Mitchell and Keith Smith

MP Middleton Press

Cover pictures: Class O2 no. 34 Newport was pictured aptly at Newport on 18th May 1952, still wearing the early style of BR livery. Semaphore signals were still in use on the modernised railway at Ryde St. Johns Road when unit no. 044 was photographed on 24th August 1981. (P.Hay and T.Heavyside)

Published April 1998

ISBN 1 901706 12 5

© *Middleton Press, 1998*

Design Deborah Goodridge

Published by
 Middleton Press
 Easebourne Lane
 Midhurst, West Sussex
 GU29 9AZ
Tel: 01730 813169
Fax: 01730 812601

Printed & bound by Biddles Ltd,
 Guildford and Kings Lynn

CONTENTS

INDEX

MAPS AND DIAGRAMS

ACKNOWLEDGEMENTS

We are very grateful for the assistance received from many of the photographers mentioned in the captions and also for invaluable help given by D.Brown, N.L.Browne, R.M.Casserley, T.Cooper, G.Croughton, J.Edgington, E.W.Fry, M.King, J.R.W.Kirkby, N.Langridge, R.Newman, Mr D. & Dr S. Salter, R.Silsbury, D.Walker and our very supportive wives.

GEOGRAPHICAL SETTING

The railway from Ryde to Ventnor first crosses the undulating northern plain, composed of marls and gravels and at Brading it joins the valley of the tiny River Yar, which passes through a gap in the Downs that form the spine of the Island. The once important harbour at St. Helens is at the mouth of this river.

The Sandown area is, not surprisingly, a region of fairly level sand, which continues to Shanklin. Thereafter, the line climbed steeply through Sandrock Beds and crossed an area of gault clay at Wroxall before penetrating the chalk mass of South Wight to reach Ventnor.

The Cowes to Sandown line followed the broad, almost level, valley of the River Medina as far as Newport. At this place the valley cuts through the central Chalk ridge of the island and the line ran parallel to the now tiny River Medina as far as Blackwater, continuing close to one of its tributaries almost to Merstone Junction. Here the watershed was crossed, the railway then running down the shallow valley of the River Yar until turning sharply out of it, just before reaching Sandown. The Ventnor West branch from Merstone Junction climbed along the upper part of the valley of the small River Yar, passing its source close to the entrance to the tunnel. This tunnel pierced the chalk mass of the Southern Downs and brought the line out onto a shelf on the cliffs of the south coast, along which it continued to its terminus.

The Ryde to Freshwater route ran roughly parallel to the central Chalk ridge, across the very undulating northern lowlands. Upon reaching Yarmouth the line joined the extremely short valley of the western River Yar to reach the terminus at Freshwater.

Ordnance Survey maps are at the scale of 1 inch to 1 mile and are from the 1947 revision; north is at the top.

The track diagrams show the final layout in the steam era and are reproduced by permission of the Signalling Record Society. Their publication "The Signalling of the Isle of Wight Railways" gives a detailed explanation of the lever numbers shown herein.

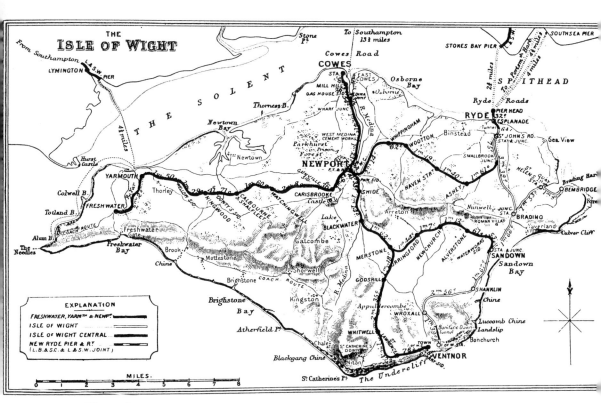

The Railway Clearing House map of 1914 indicates the owning companies at that time.

HISTORICAL BACKGROUND

The dates of opening are listed below, the 1900 company names being shown on the map.

16 June 1862	Cowes to Newport
23 August 1864	Ryde St. Johns Rd. to Shanklin
15 September 1866	Shanklin to Ventnor
1 February 1875	Sandown to Shide
20 December 1875	Smallbrook Jn. to Newport
1 June 1879	Shide to Newport (in stages)
5 April 1880	Ryde St. Johns Rd. to Esplanade
12 July 1880	Ryde Esplanade to Pier Head
27 May 1882	Brading to Bembridge
10 September 1888	Newport to Freshwater (goods)
19 July 1889	Newport to Freshwater (passengers)
20 July 1897	Merstone to St. Lawrence
1 June 1900	St. Lawrence to Ventnor Town (West later)

The lines all became part of the Southern Railway in 1923 and were nationalised on 1st January 1948, the year in which this volume commences.

Closures

15 September 1952	Merstone - Ventnor West
21 September 1953	Newport - Freshwater, also Brading - Bembridge
6 February 1956	Newport - Sandown
21 February 1966	Cowes - Smallbrook Junction.
18 April 1966	Shanklin - Ventnor

Electrification

Closed on 1st January 1967, the Ryde Pier Head - Shanklin section saw electric services introduced on 20th March 1967. A 630 volt DC third rail system was employed, using redundant London Transport tube stock.

Recent History

The Wight Locomotive Society was formed in 1966 to rescue a class O2 0-4-4T for static display. Plans were changed and eventually six of the Island's coaches were saved as well. No. 24 *Calbourne* was selected and stored at Ryde St. John's Road until 15th August 1969, when it was moved by road to Newport to join the coaches and other items of rolling stock. The track between Haven Street and Wootton was acquired, the land being leased from the county council. All stock was moved to Haven Street on 27th January 1971 and the Isle of Wight Railway Company was formed in 1972.

A loop at Wootton was brought into use on 21st August 1977, but the new platform had to wait until 31st May 1987. Extension eastwards to a new station at Smallbrook Junction took place on 20th July 1991.

Meanwhile, the British Rail line had become part of Network SouthEast in 1986. It remained thus until 1st April 1994, when it was rebranded "Island Line" in preparation for privatisation. This took place on 13th October 1996, when the entire railway operation was franchised to Stagecoach and controlled from their bus offices at Lewes.

LOCOMOTIVES

Present on the Island at the time of nationalisation were three classes of engine. (There were also about 100 coaches and 500 wooden-bodied wagons.)

Class O2 0-4-4Ts were represented by nos. 14 to 34 inclusive. Nos 35 and 36 arrived in 1949.

Class A1X "Terrier" 0-6-0Ts were two in total; nos 8 and 13. Both were returned to the mainland in 1949 for further use on the Hayling Island branch.

Class E1 0-6-0Ts were four in number. They had been provided for the heavy coal trains from Medina Wharf and were numbered 1 to 4. They were all withdrawn between 1957 and 1960.

By the end of 1966, only 11 engines were serviceable, these including no. 24 *Calbourne*, earmarked for preservation.

SECTION 1 - STEAM LEGACY

RYDE TO VENTNOR

RYDE PIER HEAD

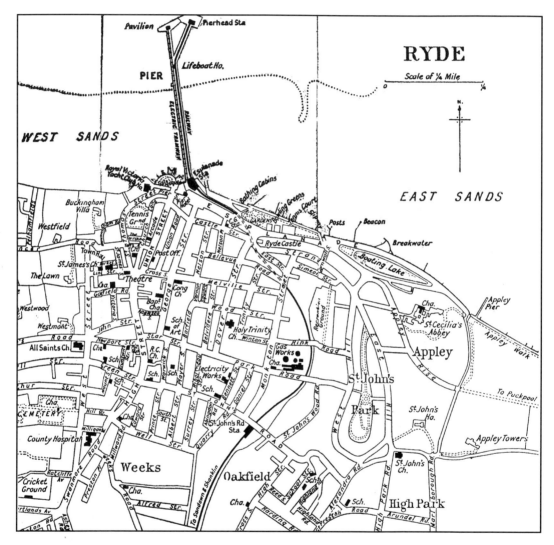

I. A guide book map from the 1920s shows the relationship of the three Ryde stations. Little has changed since, except that the ELECTRIC TRAMWAY became petrol driven in 1927.

II. The route indicator exhibited platform numbers.

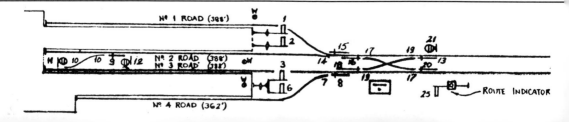

1. No. 36 *Carisbrooke* waits to depart on 4th August 1954, while the paddle steamer Ryde is berthed on the right. This vessel was sold in 1970 to become a nightclub on the Medina. (T.Wright)

2. The motor vessels *Southsea* and *Brading* maintained the link with Portsmouth Harbour until catamarans were introduced in 1987/88. A June 1962 photograph shows one of the two pairs of Drewry trams and a train ready to depart from platform 1. **Change:** see pictures 70-72. (C.L.Caddy)

RYDE ESPLANADE

3. The tramway had two independent tracks with platforms both sides for speedy loading and discharging. Shoulder to shoulder packing was practised at peak times but closure took place in January 1969. The cars had their petrol engines replaced by diesels in 1959-60. (E.Wilmshurst)

4. A 1962 northward view includes a tram in its platform. The tramway had run across the streets to the St. Johns Road station until 1880; the replacement railway could not avoid having this severe curvature on the coast line. It has been an operating nuisance ever since. **Change:** see pictures 73-74. (C.L.Caddy)

5. The 1880 route was only just below road level, as can be seen on 25th May 1966 as no. 20 *Shanklin* arrives with the 14.55 from Shanklin. The limited headroom was reduced much further during the electrification preparations, partly to improve drainage arrangements. The associated pumps are in the building to the right of no. 20. (T.Heavyside)

6. No. 14 *Fishbourne* was recorded on 25th May 1966 working the 13.19 Ryde Pier Head to Shanklin. During the final months of the Cowes service, such trains started from the loop platform on the right. The maximum number of coaches on that route was five (officially) but only four if running to platform 2 at Cowes. (T.Heavyside)

7. The locomotive shed (right) was adjacent to the up platform and was in use until the end of steam operation. No. 31 *Chale* and no. 20 *Shanklin* were pictured in May 1966, with the coal stage in the background. The entire site was cleared later. The steam locomotive fleet was the last on BR to use air braking; the Westinghouse steam pumps are on the side of the smokeboxes. (T.Heavyside)

8. Ryde Works was adjacent to the down loop and undertook all locomotive and coach repair work, the latter after the closure of Newport Works in 1924. No. 16 *Ventnor* was under the hoist on 16th July 1963, while a wagon has body surgery and a coach has bogie therapy. **Change:** see pictures 76-83. (C.L.Caddy)

III. The diagram reveals the seasonal variation in track use south of the station.

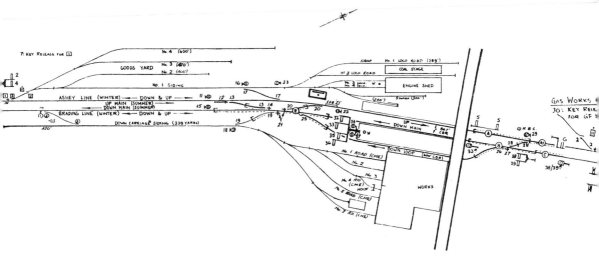

9. South of the station, no. 29 *Alverstone* was pictured working a train to Cowes on 21st September 1964. The Summer timetable had ended on 6th of that month and so two single lines were in operation for the ensuing months. The right hand distant signal arm was removed during the Summer timetable. The huts were for use by fogmen. (M.Dart coll.)

SMALLBROOK JUNCTION

IV. The diagram shows the Summer arrangement. The signal box was closed during the Winter and the junction ceased to exist operationally.

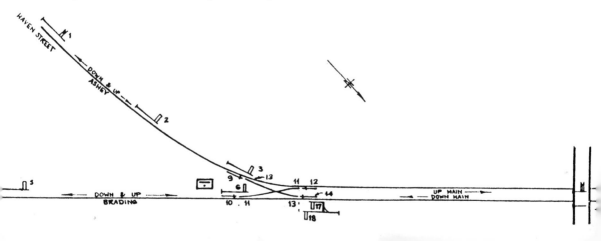

10. The signalman returns to his box with the key token on 9th September 1965, as no. 20 *Shanklin* leaves the single line from Brading. He had a 20-lever knee frame but no mains services - water was brought by train in cans. Upon electrification the junction became a single point electrically operated from Ryde St. John's Road box. **Change:** see pictures 84 and 118-120. (J.Scrace)

BRADING

PASSENGERS
MUST CROSS LINE
BY THE BRIDGE

11. A northward view in June 1949 includes the Bembridge branch in the background, to the left of the locomotive. This is no. 14 *Fishbourne*, which has just run round the branch train. On the ground is a steel replacement for the all-timber original IWR starting signals. (Wessex coll.)

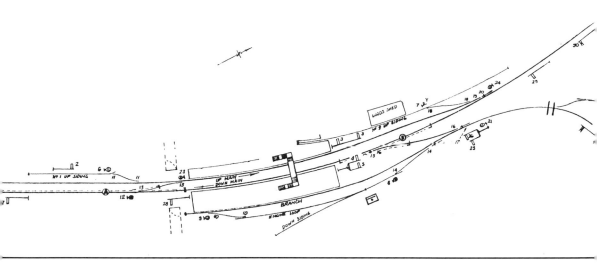

V. Top right is the line from Ryde and below it is the Bembridge branch. The siding on it served a cement works. Although the branch closed on 21st September 1953, the line to St. Helens Quay was not officially taken out of use until 17th November 1957, it being used for the transfer of condemned stock. This was cut up on the quay, the scrap being sent away by sea.

12. Another northward panorama, but from July 1963, shows the signal box standing in splendid isolation. Most of its 30 levers were disused by that time. There was to be little change here during the following 25 years - even the gas lights remained in use. **Change:** see pictures 85-87. (C.L.Caddy)

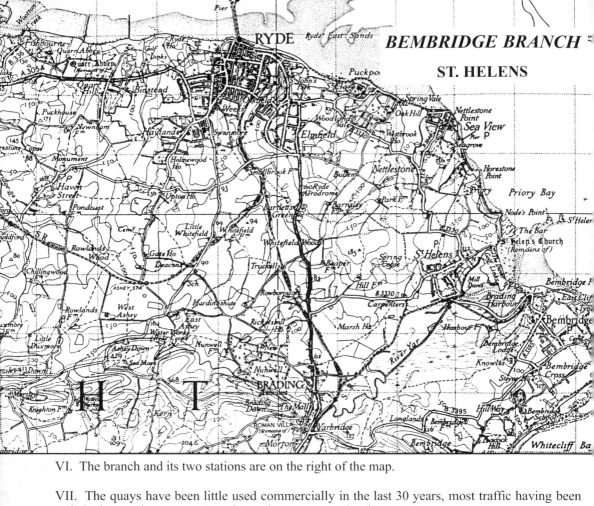

BEMBRIDGE BRANCH

ST. HELENS

VI. The branch and its two stations are on the right of the map.

VII. The quays have been little used commercially in the last 30 years, most traffic having been switched to road transport. A yacht marina now occupies the area.

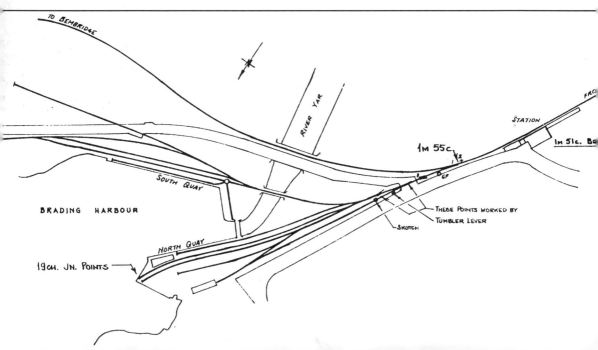

TO BEMBRIDGE

RIVER YAR

STATION

1M 55c.

1M 51c. B
FRO

BRADING HARBOUR

SOUTH QUAY

NORTH QUAY

19cH. JN. POINTS

THESE POINTS WORKED BY TUMBLER LEVER

SKOTCH

GP

13. Looking towards Bembridge in 1953, we see the line curving to the right. The track to the quays passed under the loading gauge and over the toll road at the level crossing gates. **Change:** private dwelling. (N.W.Sprinks)

BEMBRIDGE

14. As at St. Helens, a substantial building was provided and few alterations were made during the life of the branch. An exception was the turntable (foreground), which had been replaced in 1936. (Lens of Sutton)

15. The turntable functioned as a sector plate, giving the locomotive a few degrees turn to gain access to the loop. It remained in use until the branch closed on 21st September 1953. No. 14 *Fishbourne* was photographed a year earlier. (H.C.Casserley)

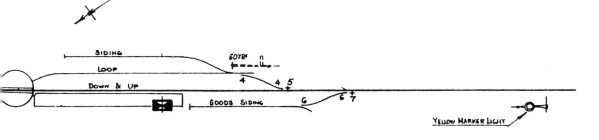

SIDING

LOOP

DOWN & UP

GOODS SIDING

60YS

4

4 5

6

6 7

YELLOW MARKER LIGHT

VIII. There were no signals on the branch and only two ground frames.

16. The ground frame was housed in the former signal box, which is partially obscured by the long canopy. Only five of the ten levers were in use. Ash up to the rail top and a spare coach complete this 1953 portrait of a peaceful terminus. **Change:** site redeveloped for yachtsmen's cottages. (N.W.Sprinks)

BEMBRIDGE

SANDOWN

17. No. 3 *Ryde* waits with the afternoon school train to Cowes on a wet January day in 1956. The line to the right of the train was used as a locomotive run round loop. (T.Wright)

IX. The route from Brading is on the left and the single line from Newport at the bottom.

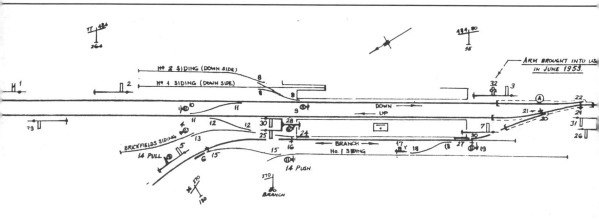

18. Standing at the down platform on 25th May 1966 is no. 20 *Shanklin*, with a train of well groomed coaches. Although noted for its holiday crowds, the station regularly handled large numbers of pupils from a nearby school. **Change:** see pictures 88-92. (T.Heavyside)

SHANKLIN

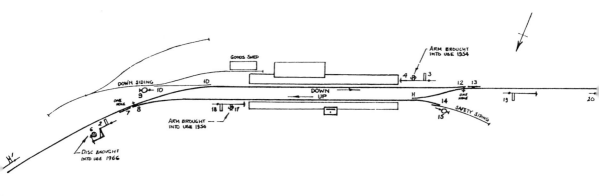

X. The diagram has the single line from Sandown on the left and shows two signalling improvements.

19. Ventnor bound on 16th July 1963 is no. 17 *Seaview*. The 1954 shunt signal allowed locomotives of terminating trains to run round. (C.L.Caddy)

20. There were no signs of the impending electrification when the north end of the station was photographed on 10th September 1966. A luggage van stands in the dock; this would be the last year of their use. **Change:** see pictures 94-95. (C.L.Caddy)

21. The station reverted to being a terminus on 18th April 1966 and Southern Vectis provided a road link from the station to Ventnor. A new Bristol MW was working the route on 10th September 1966. The service was withdrawn in May 1983. Ventnor residents campaigned hard for rail reinstatement in the early 1990s but were unsuccessful. (C.L.Caddy)

WROXALL

22. The Locomotive Club of Great Britain organised a railtour on 3rd October 1965. No. 24 *Calbourne* blows off as it is prepared for the 1 in 88 climb to the tunnel under St. Boniface Down. No. 14 *Fishbourne* is the train engine. The same club ran a farewell trip on 31st December 1966 using *Calbourne* and *Chale*. **Change:** the area has been redeveloped for housing. (M.Dart coll.)

XI. A 10-lever frame was provided on the up platform, adjacent to the booking office so that one man could perform two functions.

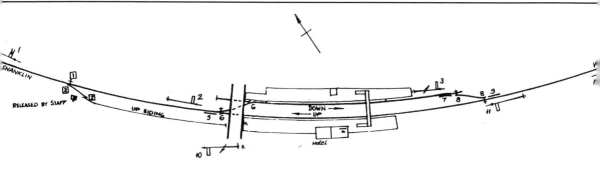

VENTNOR

23. The mass of St. Boniface Down dominates the background as the fireman closes the smokebox door of no. 36 *Carisbrooke* on 12th August 1960. The tunnel mouth is to the left of the water column.. (T.Wright)

XII. The signs in the tunnel were to guide drivers where to stop during shunting movements. Delays had ensued when the train had come to a stand fouling the points.

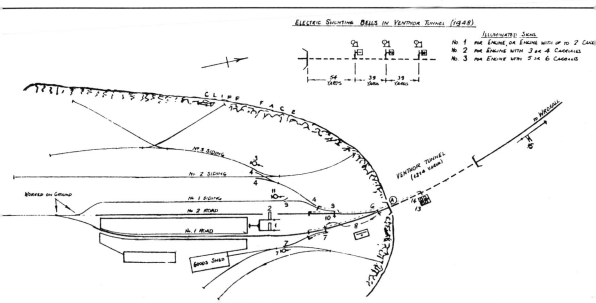

24. No. 27 *Merstone* was pictured on no. 1 road on 19th June 1965. This line had the unusual feature of what was officially described as "a portable footbridge" for use when the island platform was needed. The caves were used for storage. **Change:** the plot is now an industrial estate. (C.L.Caddy)

25. The driver of no. 32 *Bonchurch* accepts the key token which had replaced the electric train staff system in 1957. The down signals in the tunnel were of the colour light type in the final years. The box had 15 levers and all but three were in use. (A.A.F.Bell)

SMALLBROOK JUNCTION TO COWES

SMALLBROOK JUNCTION

26. We start our journey on the Island's other main line by witnessing a train from Cowes approaching the junction on 7th June 1954. The signalman is ready to accept the token. Although passenger services to Cowes were withdrawn on 21st February 1966, the line remained open until the end of the year for engineers trains. "One engine in steam" was allowed and it had to carry a special wooden staff. (Pamlin Prints)

ASHEY

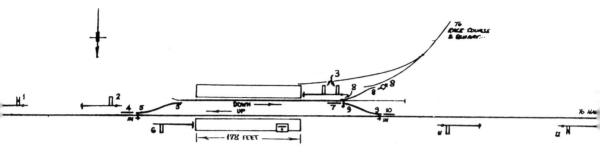

XIII. Many changes took place here during the last 50 years. The line to the race course (top) was removed in about 1926.

27. A 1953 photograph shows the former loop in use as a siding, the western connection having been removed in 1926. Mobile clay caused the signboard to move; the platform soon did likewise. Consequently the siding was abolished and the running line moved from the up to the down platform in 1961. Staffing ceased in 1953 and the 10-lever signal box frame was replaced by a ground frame in 1956. **Change:** station bulding is a private house. Down platform in use again. (J.H.Aston)

HAVEN STREET

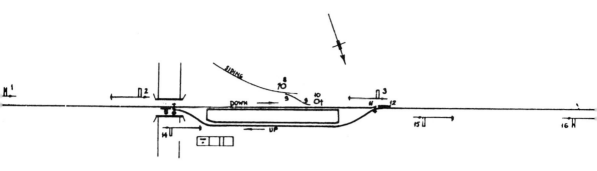

XIV. Between the installation of a loop by the SR in 1926 and closure of the station by BR in 1966, very little changed here, apart from the siding which was removed in about 1960. The station and village name was officially two words from 9th June 1958, although the station signs were not changed immediately.

28. Trains usually passed here every hour throughout the day in the Summer. No. 33 *Bembridge* is waiting to proceed to Cowes on 5th August 1965. The siding had been used for coal for the village gasworks (right) until its closure in the 1920s. (R.E.Ruffell)

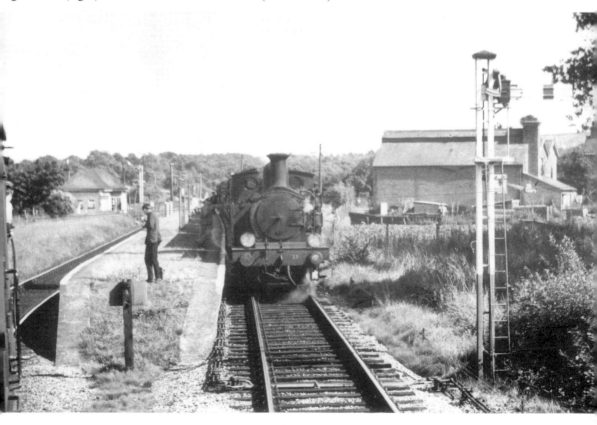

29. Since the closure of Ryde Gasworks in about 1955, most of the coal imported at Medina Wharf was for heating and locomotive purposes. No. 28 *Ashey* departs for Ryde on 16th February 1966. A 16-lever frame was installed adjacent to the ticket office for one-man operation. **Change:** see pictures 98-107. (T.Wright)

WOOTTON

30. This station was on the opposite side of the road to the present one and had no buildings, the booking office being in one of the arches of the road bridge from under which this picture was taken in 1953. An inclined path, with one reversal, led up to the road on the other side of which there was a single siding. This was used by coal merchant Osborn until 1959. Passenger traffic ceased at this station and at Whippingham on 21st September 1953. **Change:** cutting infilled due to land movement. (J.H.Aston)

WHIPPINGHAM

31. Reputed to have had a private waiting room for Queen Victoria, the station saw very little traffic. The rodding tunnel can be seen; this led to an 11-lever frame, which was taken out of use on 6th February 1956. **Change:** private house. (H.C.Casserley)

XV. The up loop was abandoned in 1956, after which time trains took the direct line through the down platform.

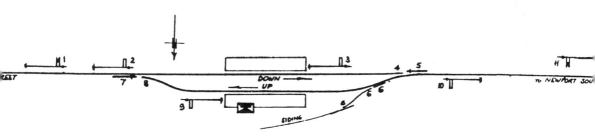

NEWPORT

32. Looking east from the station footbridge, we witness the arrival of a train from Ryde on 9th August 1965, headed by no. 22 *Brading*. It is on the drawbridge over the River Medina; a similar parallel span had been situated to the right of it for the Sandown trains, which were withdrawn in 1956. (T.Wright)

XVI. The diagram indicates the location of the 20-lever Newport South box. It remained in use until 23rd March 1958, by which time the trackwork had been simplified as seen in picture 32.

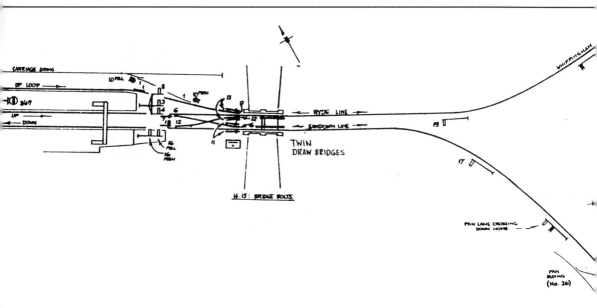

33. No. 20 *Shanklin* rumbles over the remaining spans on its way to Cowes on 18th September 1965. Considerable labour was required to unbolt fishplates, disconnect signal wires, lower one end of each span, winch them back and then reverse the process. (E.Wilmshurst)

34. Reverting to August 1953, we can admire no. 26 *Whitwell* departing for Sandown, under the impressive array of starting signals. The connection on the extreme right was to the carriage siding. (D.Trevor Rowe)

35. A 1962 panorama of the Cowes end of the station includes a van in the down bay, the platform once used by Freshwater trains. The banner repeater indicated the aspect of the obscured starting signal. (C.L.Caddy)

XVII. The Freshwater branch is at the bottom of the North Box diagram. "Slotted by South" meant that these signals were jointly worked with South Box.

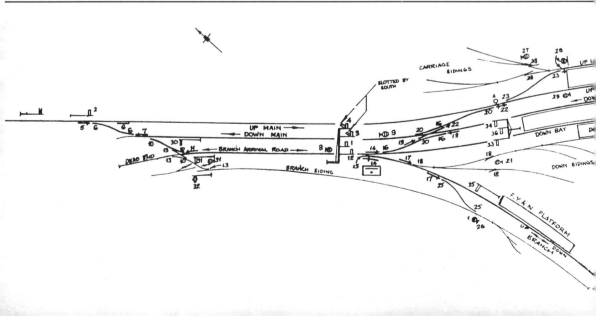

36. A long train of locomotive coal is about to leave for Ryde St. Johns Road at 12.07 on 9th August 1965 from the branch arrival road. The box had a 36-lever frame and was designated "North Box" until 1958. The locomotive is no. 20 *Shanklin*. **Change:** site used for a bypass road. (E.Wilmshurst)

37. Evident in this photograph from April 1967 is the back of the signal box and the roof of the carriage repair shop, which had been in use until November 1957. Awaiting scrapping on the former Freshwater branch are nos 27, 16, 20, 35, 28, 17, 33, 14 and 22. The heavily patched wagons were also about to succumb to the scrap merchants. (E.Wilmshurst)

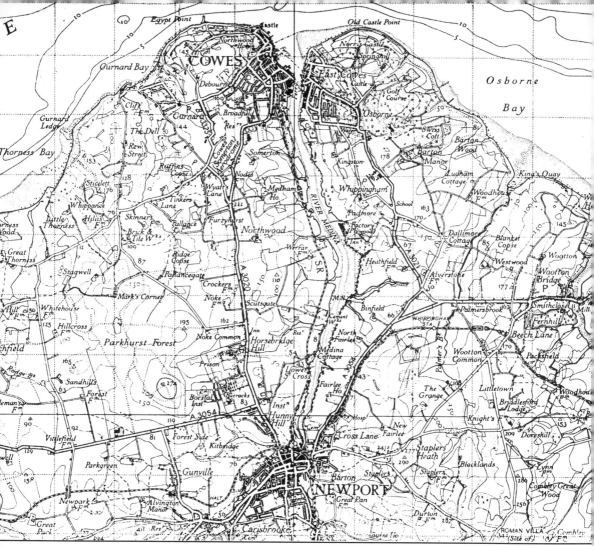

XVIII. Wootton station is on the right, near the words "Beech Lane". Whippingham is to the left of it, more than two miles south of the former royal residence at Osborne. The line to Freshwater is on the left and is shown as far as Watchingwell.

CEMENT MILLS HALT

38. The short platform is viewed from the south in February 1966. Originally intended for workers, in later years it was occasionally used by fishermen, printed tickets being available from Cowes, Mill Hill and Newport. The siding received chalk from Shide until 1944. **Change:** little trace now. (T.Wright)

MEDINA WHARF

39. No. 24 *Calbourne* climbs up the 1 in 60 gradient from the waterfront on 9th August 1965 to join the line from Cowes. A ground frame and intermediate key token instrument were situated here. (T.Wright)

XIX. The line from Newport is on the right.

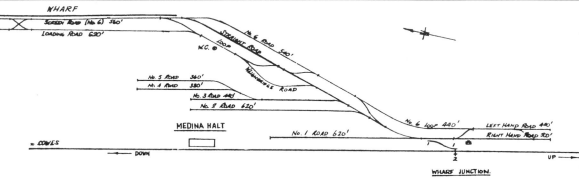

40. On the left are four storage sidings; in the centre is the weigh-house, which is dwarfed by the water tower and in the left background is one of the two travelling conveyors. There had been a good crop of grass in 1965. **Change:** private commercial property. (A.E.Bennett)

41. The two massive travelling cranes are evident, as are the capstans used for rope haulage of wagons under the loading bins. *Allard* was also the name of a speedy sports car in the previous decade. (E.Wilmshurst)

42. The location of Medina Halt is shown on the diagram; it was built for the benefit of wharf workers. In the distance is a van on no. 1 siding. The footpath to the wharf is obscured by the platform. (Lens of Sutton)

MILL HILL

43. Well situated in the populous southern part of Cowes, the station was able to produce impressive passenger figures. There was no goods yard, but a siding to the south was used by a coal merchant until 1965. This is a northward view in 1966. **Change:** The site was developed for housing in 1996. (T.Wright)

COWES

44. Cramped, steeply graded and curved, the terminus was far from ideal. Standing at platlform 1, adjacent to the coal siding, on 9th August 1965 is no. 22 *Brading*, ready to leave with five coaches.(T.Wright)

XX. Although signalled for departure of passenger workings, the short platform 3 was used only once a day by an early morning train.

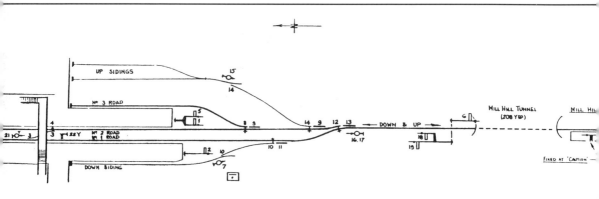

45. After arrival, the empty train was usually propelled onto this length of track and braked. The locomotive ran forward, reversed over the crossover and the guard then ran the coaches under gravity back to the platform. All except one of the box's 22 levers were in use. (A.E.Bennett)

46. Crowds wait on the concourse on 9th August 1965 for the run-round to take place. The mail train is berthed in platform 2. The bridge from which this picture was taken carried a public footpath and was dismantled for reuse on the Mid-Hants Railway at Medstead & Four Marks. **Change:** part of the site was used for a bus terminus but most lay idle for about 30 years before being occupied predominantly by a super-market. (T.Wright)

FRESHWATER BRANCH

WEST OF NEWPORT

47. Our trip on the branch starts on the edge of Newport, behind no. 27 *Merstone*. Our train, having rounded the curve seen in picture 37, will have just crossed the nine brick arches of the viaduct. Part of the viaduct spanned the road to Cowes at Hunny Hill. **Change:** All was lost by 1996, except for part of the brick section of the viaduct. (D.Trevor Rowe)

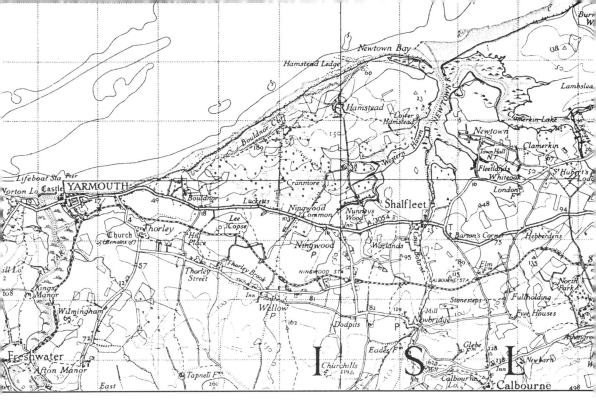

XXI. The right border continues from map XVIII in the vicinity of Watchingwell.

CARISBROOKE

48. A second 1953 photograph and this is a westward view. The white gate is on the line to the goods yard which, although overgrown and disused, was officially still open. The up loop had long gone and had only been used for running round in its final years. (J.H.Aston)

49. Originally a private station, it remained open and well kept to the end.
Evident in 1953 are the levers that controlled two signals. The single siding
was behind the far end of the platform. **Change:** Still extant. (J.H.Aston)

CALBOURNE

50. Evident are the changed signal arms (upper quadrant) but unchanged posts (LSWR left - SR right). Hand worked gates, oil lamps and trim gardens were things of the past on much of the mainland. Here also there was one siding behind the platform. **Change:** Bungalow on the site. (R.Silsbury coll.)

NINGWOOD

51. A passing loop was provided here together wiith a nine-lever framed signal box (by the left pole), one siding (extreme left) and a water tank (right). **Change:** Converted to a dwelling. (Lens of Sutton)

YARMOUTH

52. The down platform and loop had long gone from the foreground when this photograph was taken in the final year of operation. Many of the residents of the fine houses in Station Road would miss the convenient route to the Island's capital. (Pamlin Prints)

53. Two years after closure, little had altered. The gate on the left had given access to the solitary goods siding. **Change:** The building was converted to a youth club. (A.E.Bennett)

FRESHWATER

54. No book on Island lines is complete without mention of the popular named train whch ran between Freshwater and Ventnor in the Summers of the peacetime years from 1934 to 1953. Only one coach had a toilet and this had to be locked at Wroxall to ensure that Ventnor's water was not contaminated, the supply originating mainly in the tunnel. (J.H.Aston)

55. September 1952 and holidaymaker's luggage waits for a train to follow them home. Such traffic was big business on the Island lines, many vans being dedicated to it. The box had a 10-lever frame and was moved outside the station after closure to serve as a bus shelter before reverting to its intended function at Wootton on the IOWSR. (A.J.Pike/F.Hornby)

56. The exterior was photographed in 1962 when the signs read LADIES and GENTLEMEN. The facilities were maintained by the local authority. **Change:** The building was replaced by a spring factory; this in turn was demolished in favour of a supermarket and garden centre. (C.L.Caddy)

XXII. The revised signal box position meant that it could be worked by station staff.

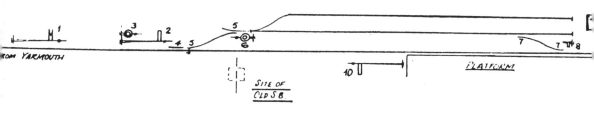

NEWPORT TO SANDOWN

XXIII. This entire route is shown opposite, together with the two routes to Ventnor and also the Smallbrook Junction to Newport line.

SHIDE

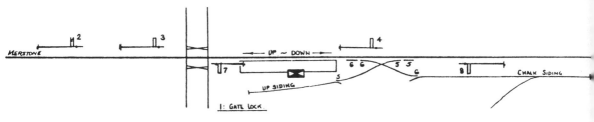

XXIV. Trains had to reverse from the chalk siding to the quarry where gravel was also loaded.

57. Looking south in January 1956, we have the sidings out of view at our left hand and a 9-lever signal box centre stage. This was a block post with key token instruments which allowed goods trains to be worked thus far and locked into the sidings. **Change:** Site occupied by a tyre service centre and the diverted river is in the place of the trackbed. (T.Wright)

BLACKWATER

58. The level crossing on the A3020 is behind us, as is the single siding. Looking like a black pillar is a stretcher cupboard, a feature of most stations in 1956. **Change:** The house has been extended and the platform is still evident. (E.Wilmshurst)

MERSTONE

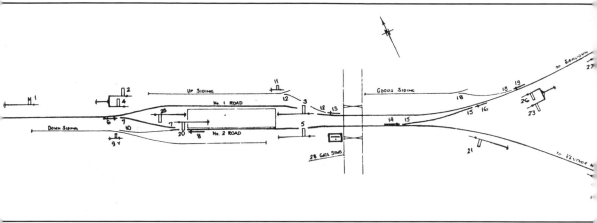

XXV. The note GATE STOPS indicates that the level crossing gates were wheel-operated, the only example on the island.

59. Traffic was slim on a wet day in January 1956 as no. 29 *Alverstone* pauses with its train for Sandown. The path led to two uncontrolled wicket gates. The train on the left is bound for Cowes behind no. 33 *Bembridge*. The junction can be seen in picture 64. (T.Wright)

HORRINGFORD

60.   There was one siding here; it terminated behind the sign on the right and was much used for sugar beet in the final years. The box housed five levers used in connection with gate protection. **Change:** converted to a house with two large dormer windows added. (S.C.Nash)

NEWCHURCH

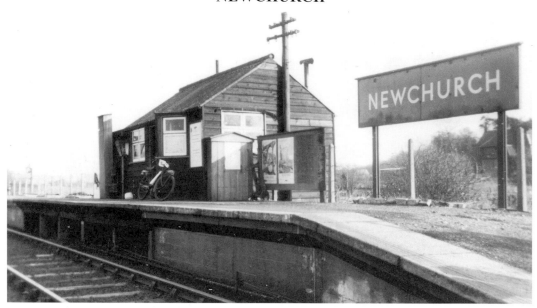

61. As at Blackwater a hut replaced the original building and there was another well placed stretcher cupboard. The signal wires pass under the platform to reach the six levers. The siding was opposite the platform and received substantial quantities of anthracite for production of gas for the engines at Knighton Water Works. **Change:** A bungalow was built on the site. (E.Wilmshurst)

ALVERSTONE

62. The siding was to the right of the picture and was separated from the running line by a stream. There were only two signals, both distants, worked in conjunction with the gates. **Change:** The building became a private dwelling. (E.Wilmshurst)

63. Our scenic journey along the foot of Ashey Down comes to an end as we climb up at 1 in 54 and take the curve into platform 3, seen in picture 17. We will have passed Sandown Water Works siding which was on the south of the line. (J.Chillman coll.)

VENTNOR WEST BRANCH

MERSTONE

64. The signalman walks towards no. 27 *Merstone* with the Sandown token, as a lady strolls in front of the engine on 3rd September 1952. No. 35 *Freshwater* is ready to depart for Ventnor West and pass the 28-lever box. **Change:** The area became a highway depot, the platform being used for material storage. (H.C.Casserley)

GODSHILL

65. It seems that nothing ever changed here during the life of the railway - this and the next three pictures are probably more than 50 years old but it matters not. **Change:** Residential use. (G.Hunt/IOWSR)

WHITWELL

66. The loop was lifted in 1928, but two sidings were retained behind the station. Until 1949, branch services were usually worked by a "Terrier" 0-6-0T, as seen here. **Change:** This is now a fine dwelling with holiday accommodation. Even the up waiting shelter has been restored. (G.Hunt/IOWSR)

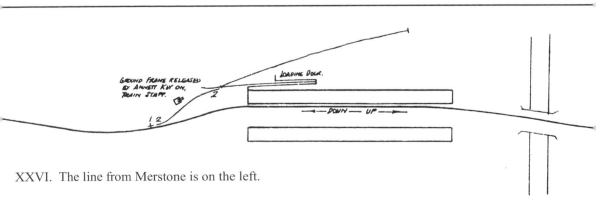

XXVI. The line from Merstone is on the left.

ST. LAWRENCE

67. Having climbed at 1 in 90 from Whitwell to St. Lawrence Tunnel, the line descended at mostly 1 in 55 to Ventnor West. Here we look towards the terminus at the lofty station building and the steep road which passes behind the fence and then over the bridge. **Change:** Residential use. (J.Chillman coll.)

VENTNOR WEST

68. A panorama towards the buffer stops includes the generous platform canopy, the water column and tank, the ash pit and dock siding. **Change:** The building is now surrounded by bungalows. (J.Chillman coll.)

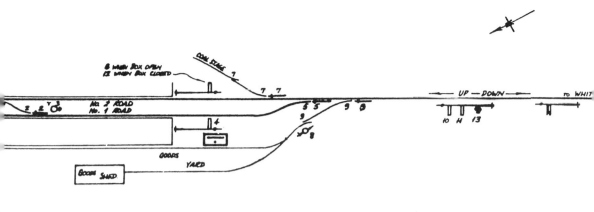

XXVII. The indistinct note by the starting signal at platform 2 was "8 when box open, 12 when box closed". Its 13 levers were usually out of use, the branch being worked "one engine in steam".

69. The exterior was recorded on the last day of service - 13th September 1952. It was staffed until that time but tickets from the intermediate stations on the branch were issued by the guard. (F.Hornby)

SECTION 2 - ELECTRIC SURVIVAL

RYDE TO SHANKLIN

RYDE PIER HEAD

70. With total closure of the remaining part of the system from 1st January to 20th March 1967, the electrification and associated engineering work could proceed speedily. Tracks 1 and 3 were removed. There were various operating patterns at different times in 1966 - single line working on the pier, Cowes trains starting at St. John's Road, Shanklin trains starting at Esplanade (using the crossover in picture 71) and finally a short shuttle train between Esplanade and St. Johns with a steam locomotive at each end, passengers using the tram on the pier. This is the scene on 7th December. Tracks were raised at all stations, except Esplanade where the platforms were lowered, as part of the curve was on land and part on the pier. (T.Wright)

71. This September 1972 view includes the 28-lever Pier Head box, which was retained in use until 5th May 1974, along with the adjacent scissors crossover. Removal of the latter, and the crossover seen here, resulted in two parallel single lines remaining. (R.E.Ruffell)

72. After 1974, the eastern single line was normally used in peak hours only to carry a shuttle service to the Esplanade, as seen on 21st July 1990. Known as "No. 2 Road", it was little used by 1996. The former platform 3 is on the right and had been retained so that passengers could be loaded on one side while unloading others from the other. (C.Wilson)

RYDE ESPLANADE

73. The route of the former tramway is evident as a seven-car train (4VEC and 3TIS) rumbles along from the Pier Head on 24th August 1981. A total of 43 vehicles was provided, running as four or seven car trains according to traffic demand. They were later reformed as five car units. The tramway station was demolished in 1996. (T.Heavyside)

74. The footbridge between the bus station and the hovercraft terminal was used to take this and the next picture. A four-set is bound for Shanklin on 7th October 1989 and passes the catch point on No. 2 Road. The former down platform canopy and building were removed in March 1978, but the subway was retained. (C.Wilson)

75. Reaching the end of the double track section on 29th August 1994 is one of the 1938-built class 483 units, introduced on 13th July 1989. All down trains use the crossover, which is operated electrically from Ryde St. John's Road. It was installed just prior to the closure of the Pier Head box. (P.G.Barnes)

76. The historic works was adapted for the maintenance of the aged electric stock built between 1924 and 1935. The initial livery was BR standard blue with high visibility yellow ends, as seen in April 1967. The units were last used on the Northern City line, between Moorgate and Finsbury Park. (E.Wilmshurst)

77. The end doors began to be plated over in 1985 - no longer could drivers try to catch pheasants in the Summer. The monotonous blue was broken with ivory panels and local logos, as witnessed in June 1986. The signal box became the only one on the route on 25th February 1989, although few of its 40 levers were in use by that time. (G.Gillham)

78. The guard peeps out of a Shanklin-bound train on 10th May 1989, as we admire the initials of the Isle of Wight Railway cast in with the tracery of the spandrels. A model railway shop occupied the booking hall in 1990-95. The new train crew room can be seen beyond the canopy. (T.Wright)

79. Spacious luggage racks (left) were fitted to the class 485/486 stock at Stewarts Lane - see picture 87 in our *Clapham Junction - 50 years of change*. Driver training took place between Wimbledon and Woking - see picture 6 in our *Woking to Southampton* album. (F.Hornby)

80. The Works had its first open day in January 1984. This is a demonstration at the Ryde Rail Festival on 21st June 1986 and one of the new BRUFF recovery vehicles is performing on its own turntable. (M.Turvey)

81. An elevated road was built in the Works as the replacement stock had underfloor electrical equipment. Upon electrification, the former down loop line (left) was converted to a siding and used for internal carriage cleaning. Shunting is in progress on 3rd November 1989, just after the first of the second generation of electric units had arrived on the Island. (C.Wilson)

82. Clinical conditions still prevailed on 1st September 1990 when two coaches were over the pit for servicing. Eight two-car units arrived in 1989-90 and another one, plus two shells, appeared in 1992, all ex-Northern Line, although originally Bakerloo stock. (C.Wilson)

83. Two spare bodies were shipped to the Isle of Wight for use as replacement cars in the event that one of the existing vehicles becomes unserviceable. The spare cars are just empty shells with windows and doors boarded up. If either vehicle were to be used then it would have to be completely fitted out internally and electrically before being put into traffic. The set has been given the theoretical number of 483010 and is viewed here as no. 483006 passes forming the 15.42 Ryde Pier Head to Shanklin on 4th May 1992. (C.Wilson)

SMALLBROOK JUNCTION

84. The station is open only when steam trains are operating, hence the need for indication on the train from Pier Head on 22nd September 1994. There is no pedestrian access to the platforms, which came into use on 20th July 1991. See also picture 118. (T.Heavyside)

85. A southward view in May 1985 includes a solitary semaphore signal and waste land where Bembridge trains had once run. The signal box closed on 28th October 1988, when the line to Sandown was singled. (V.Mitchell)

86. Looking towards Ryde in May 1989, the original owner's initials could still be seen under the canopy. Sadly other initials were periodically sprayed on the brickwork . The building was sold that year and leased to Brading Town Trust for community purposes. (T.Wright)

87. School pupils leave a four-car train on 22nd September 1994. Bridge 25 stands defiantly devoid of passengers. Gas lighting ceased in October 1986; the electric replacements were of a similar style but the bowls were more pointed. (T.Heavyside)

88. Conductor rail was landed at Medina Wharf and brought by rail during 1966 to be stacked here. It is being loaded by a hired crane on a dull December day for transport at night prior to installation. A pile of mailbags is evident on the down platform - this was another source of revenue to be lost. (T.Wright)

89. Diesel no. 05001 was recorded on 24th May 1975, berthed with engineering stock in platform 3, still so numbered nearly 20 years after the last train had left for Newport. Built in 1955, the locomotive's height was reduced prior to shipping to the Island in 1966 for use with engineering trains. It is unclear how *Nuclear Fred* became its unofficial name. (R.E.Ruffell)

90. As part of the Ryde Rail Festival on 21st June 1986, brake van rides were given behind no. 03079. Brickfield siding runs straight ahead; the former Newport route curved to the left. (M.Turvey)

91. Two four-car trains pass on 27th September 1989, bearing Network SouthEast logos. Although singling of the line from Brading had taken place in October 1988, the 32-lever framed signal box here remained in use until 25th February 1989, although with a temporary panel. (C.Wilson)

92. Built at Doncaster in 1960, no. 03079 replaced no. 05001 in 1984 and is seen on 27th September 1989 with two redundant cars. Several were hoisted onto the road vehicles that were delivering the replacements and were returned to the mainland for disposal. Five of the best were sold back to London Transport to form a vintage unit. (C.Wilson)

LAKE

93. After decades of agitation, the residents of Lake were rewarded with a station on 11th May 1987. There were unauthorised occupants in the cab as a train arrives from Shanklin in August 1990. (C.Wilson)

SHANKLIN

94. Initially, both platform lines were electrified, as seen in this March 1974 northward view. The 20-lever framed signal box (centre) was closed in July 1979. The box and up platform were demolished in July 1980 and the up line was removed. Note that part of the motor cars of the early stock was occupied by electrical equipment and earned no revenue. (R.E.Ruffell)

95. The canopy was shortened in Feruary 1978. The remaining platform was reduced at its south end and lengthened at its other end in 1979, when the bridge over the road was removed. An unattended train ran away on 21st January 1991 and subsequently the station was closed while the track was set level. (T.Wright)

SECTION 3 - STEAM REVIVAL

DEPARTURE FROM NEWPORT

96. The WLS undertook restoration work on its stock at Newport during 1967-70, but had to vacate the site at short notice on 24th January 1971. No. 24 *Calbourne* takes water prior to its second trip to Haven Street that day with the assorted stock standing in platform 2. The water tank was moved to Haven Street later. (I.Whitlam)

The Move
Richard Newman

The 4-year sojourn at Newport had been longer than originally anticipated when we bought the stock, but standard gauge railway preservation was still uncharted territory. No longer were we awaiting the deliberations of others: "The Move" marked the start of our being able to set out to chart ourown destiny. We left behind a welter of sidings for a site with no sidings, and the only services being running water and a cess pit.

At about 10.40, Calbourne ran up the yard and coupled up to three carriages which were then hauled through the Up platform on to the Viaduct for an preliminary test run, after which water had been taken. As no difficulty was apparent, the train picked up the "passengers" who had been standing patiently on the Down platform. Travel on the train had been restricted

to Society members and special guests, and indemnity forms were thus prepared for completion by all who wished to make the journey.

And so, with a blast on the guard's whistle from David Ferry, acknowledged by a "hoot" from the engine, we were away - although slight delay was experienced in persuading a small dog not to stand on the track. As we crossed the viaduct and ran into the tunnel beneath Fairlee Road, it seemed almost as if trains never stopped ruriing - except for the crowds! At every vantage point along the line, there appeared a sea of faces - many local residents of course as the enthusiast world in general had not heard of the manoeuvre. A Society member in Fairlee Road added to the event by displaying a large green flag and Union Jack from his garden! Progressup the bank was excellent - over Halberry House and Mews Lane

Crossings and through the avenue of pine trees towards Whippingham to prepare for the steepest gradient of all.

As we reached the summit of Wootton Bank, the train was brought to a stand on wet rails in the depths of the damp cutting - which is never penetrated by sunlight in winter. This was done intentionally prior to crossing the slip. Former loco foreman Ivor Davis and "operating officer" George Wheeler clambered down from the engine and with Terry Hastings and Kim Chalkley, who had positioned themselves at the cutting, they anxiously watched as the engine was coaxed inch by inch past the embankment slip, which had been further swollen by the torrential rain of the previous 24 hours. The engine and carriages were gradually eased over the buckled track, witnessed by further crowds watching from Station Road Bridge. The most difficult part of the run had been successfully accomplished! From Wootton to Haven Street steam was cut off for the downhill run through the woods and into the station, where another large crowd of people of all age groups eagerly awaited the arrival of this special train. Few people from the village could have missed the occasion and it is said that Sunday School attendance suffered badly as a result! Following due ceremony for the Press photographers, the engine took water ready for the return "light" to Newport. The carriages were berthed beyond the road bridge to the east of the station and the engine set off, pausing only for a moment after crossing Wootton slip. What a fine sight it made as it coasted downhill over Halberry House Crossing into Newport, running bunker first into the brilliant winter sunshine.

The schedule originally planned had to be revised and it was some time before the next run was made, but the opportunity was taken to marshall the goods wagons into two trains; No.24, coupled to several loaded coal wagons and the LSW Brake Van left Newport at approx. 2.35p.m. carrying on board a despatch bag which contained a letter to Her Majesty The Queen. The document commemorated the fact that this was the last train to call at Whippingham Station, once used by guests of royalty travelling to Osborne House. As the train ground to a halt at Whippingham (closed to passengers in 1953, and now a private residence), Alderman Mark Woodnutt, the Island's M.P., was waiting to receive the despatch bag from the engine crew (Bob Hurtable and Tom Jackman) and to convey it onwards to Buckingham Palace on the following Tuesday. Society officials posed for photographs on the buffer beam of Calbourne with Ald. Woodnutt, who was then welcomed aboard the engine for the remainder of the Journey to Haven Street.

After some time the engine and Brake Van ambled through the countryside back to Newport. Little time was wasted upon reaching the station however, for daylight was fast fading. At

97. The land movement referred to in caption no. 30 is evident as no. 24 passes the site of Wootton platform later that day. Contractors commenced lifting the track from Newport the following week. (J.G.Peters/IOWSR coll.)

5.45pm, No. 24 departed from the Up platform with the three SEC carriages well-laden with another load of passengers. Accommodation was strictly limited on this set for No. 4149, the Society's most recent acquisition, was devoid of all seats, while several compartments in the other coaches had been loaded with seat cushions and other miscellania. A spirited run was made to Haven Street, where, in the darkness, passengers and onlookers one by one drifted away. One carriage (6375) had its electric lighting in working order at the start of the journey, but there was little power in the batteries and the lights grew dimmer as the train proceeded on its way.

The tram, which had been stationed at Haven Street for most of the day as 'water carrier', was sent back to Newport ahead of the engine at this time to collect the remainder of the miscellaneous equipment - which included a platform trolley and the pump used for replenishment of water supplies on the engine. Working on a time interval basis, the engine returned with caution some time later and arrived at Newport just after 7.15pm to take on water and collect the remaining items - two wagons, the 6-wheel Midland crane D429 and its match truck and the 1898 LSW van (56046). After engine and tail lamps had been found and placed in position, the train was ready to leave and, at 8.30pm by the Town Hall clock, the motley assortment of wagons, loaded with a remarkable accumulation of materials, screeched out of the Up platform behind Calbourne. A small crowd of Society members watched from the platform, cheering the train on its way. A shrill hoot from the engine, followed by a series of long blasts as 24 rumbled over the viaduct ended a 109-year association which the town of Newport has had with its railway since the inauguration of the Cowes and Newport Railway in 1862. At this hour of the evening most of the people who had watched the day's proceedings had been driven home by rain, but two ladies hurried from Quay Street to the Viaduct and waved enthusiastically as the train passed overhead. Still hooting, the engine hauled its load into the tunnel and rushed the steep gradient on the other side.

This was perhaps the most sentimental journey of all - reminiscent of many a solemn 'Last Day' - for this was the final train out of Newport; the Society had at last vacated the Island capital. No. 24 made steady progress up the bank, but a stop was made just beyond Mews Lane Crossing to inject. George Wheeler, now acting as guard, walked back along the line to protect the train in accordance with Regulations, for the tram was to follow from Newport' some 20 minutes. later. As it happened, the tram suffered. a mechanical failure on the way and was only coaxed through to Haven Street by Steve Day and John'Wenyon after repairs had been carried out using parts of the diesel pump it was carrying! Meanwhile, pressure had again increased on Calbourne to allow her to proceed. A local resident had thoughtfully provided a Tilley lamp to pinpoint the exact location of the slip at Wootton and had again sanded the wet rails to ease our passage. The vintage crane, formed into this train was considered to be the most awkward vehicle to cross the slip by virtue of its 6-wheeled rigid wheelbase but it rode the distorted track in a most satisfactory manner. With an acknowledging hoot, Calbourne ran downhill as far as the Haven Street distant signal, where a special stop was made to pin down brakes.

The rainswept woods echoed with the clanging buffers and couplings on the old wagons, and the hiss of steam from the engine as the train restarted to run the final few hundred yards into the platform, where another Tilley lamp swung from a post in the wind - a welcome signal through the darkness. At 9.50p.m. the train came to a stand at Haven Street, while the tram eventually arrived at 10.30pm, having been delayed by its mechanical troubles. Our entry into the 'White Hart' public house shortly afterwards to the strains of suitable "railway" piano music from the resident pianist proved that the villagers of Havenstreet would not forget the day that their railway "came back"!

Reproduced from *Wight Report* by kind permission of the editor.

98. Another view from the same day shows *Calbourne* having arrived with three coaches; less obvious is the chassis of the former Ryde Pier train no. 2. Almost five years since the last passenger departed, the lamp posts were still in place and the building remained intact. (J.Goss)

99. *Invincible* arrived in 1971, by which time a massive weeding operation had taken place. Built in 1915 by Hawthorn Leslie, the locomotive served at Woolwich Arsenal and the Royal Aircraft Establishment at Farnborough. She was later fitted with air brakes and worked all passenger trains in 1973-76. Over 9000 passengers were conveyed on alternate Sunday afternoons in the Summer of 1971, the first season in steam. (IOWSR coll.)

100. With stock berthed in the platform, one of the first tasks for volunteers was the installation of sidings. There was no shortage of redundant track material available for purchase from the line east of this station and west of Wootton. (C.Parish/IOWSR coll.)

101. Terrier no. 11 *Newport* returned to the Island in 1973, although she did not steam again until 1989. The photograph shows the loading at Broad Street Slipway, Portsmouth. Since this time the ferries have been replaced twice and the berth moved to Gunwharf. (J.Goss)

102. *Invincible* carried one of the largest headboards ever created. It commemorated the event described thereon on 17th August 1975, although the actual centenary was on 20th December. No opportunity has been lost to publicise the line. (J.Goss/IOWSR coll.)

103. *Calbourne* had received a major overhaul only 18 months before withdrawal but serious surgery was required in 1972-75. The locomotive was turned by a crane prior to reassembly. (Sir Peter Allen)

104. A major leap forward for the enterprising team was the erection of a workshop in 1980, after more than a decade of struggling in the elements. The official opening took place on 3rd January 1981. (I.Whitlam)

105. A panorama taken on 21st July 1985 includes no. 8 *Freshwater*, four years after its return to steam on the Island. The small headboard shows "Ryde to Ventnor", the title of our book that was launched that day. In the background is the fine buffet, which was opened on 24th July 1982. On the left is the diesel last seen in picture 89, together with a 1953 Wickham railcar. (V.Mitchell)

106. The former gas retort house had been used as a barn until purchased in May 1983 for conversion to offices. Work is seen in progress on 15th July 1985 on the new shop (with matching windows). (I.Whitlam)

107. With its experience working on the old SR Island coaches, the railway has come to the forefront of carriage restoration. Several former bungalows and garden sheds have had their dignity restored and been united with a suitable van chassis. Built in 1898, no. 4112 was last used as a push-pull coach on the Ventnor West branch in 1938. (R.MacDonald)

108. A reliable diesel locomotive was needed for the eastward extension work and also as a passenger train standby. Class 03 no. D2059 was purchased from BR and arrived on the Island on 4th November 1988. Named *Edward*, it was photographed in the following August together with one of the single bolster wagons brought to the Island in 1966 for the transport of conductor rails. The wagon was acquired by the IOWSR in 1982 and adapted for boiler wash-out purposes. (M.Turvey)

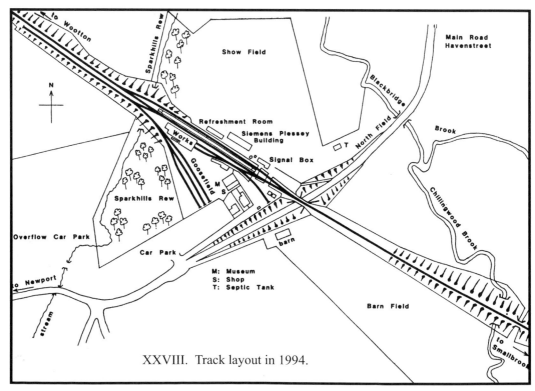

XXVIII. Track layout in 1994.

109. Not only are the coaches smart and authentic, but so are the uniforms. Guard Chalkley is justifiably proud as one of the first public trains to Smallbrook Junction is about to depart on 21st July 1991. The connection to the workshop is on the right. (V.Mitchell)

110. The connection to Goosefield Siding is on the left as no. 8 *Freshwater* approaches the other end of the platform on 29th August 1994, bound for Smallbrook Junction. Note the commendable condition of everything in view. The ex-Sandown signal was dismantled at the end of 1996 for re-erection at the east end of the station. (P.G.Barnes)

LOCOMOTIVES

W8 *Freshwater*	A1/x Class Terrier 0-6-0T (LBSC 46 *Newington*, 1876)
IWC No. 11 (alias W11 *Newport*)	A1/x Class Terrier 0-6-0T (LBSC 40 *Brighton*, 1878)
W24 *Calbourne*	O2 Class 0-4-4T (LSW 209, 1891)
W37 *Invincible*	Hawthorn Leslie 0-4-0ST (Woolwich Arsenal, 1915)
Ajax	Barclay 0-6-0T owned by H. Frampton-Jones (1918)
War Dept 198 *Royal Engineer*	Hunslet 0-6-0ST 'Austerity' owned by RCT Museum Trust (1953)
Army 235	Barclay 0-4-0DM owned by RCT Museum Trust (1945)
D2059 *Edward*	BR Class 03 0-6-0DM (BR, 1959)
D2554 *Nuclear Fred*	Hunslet Class 05 0-6-0DM (BR 11140, 1956)

PASSENGER STOCK

IWR 46	Composite (NLR, 1864; later IWR) allocated SR Island No. 6336
1046, 1052	PLV (SR, 1936 & 1943 resp.)
2416	bogie Third (LBSC, 1916)
4112	Driving Brake Saloon Third (LCD, 1898)
4145, 4149	bogie Brake Third (SEC, 1911)
4168	bogie Brake Third (LBSC, 1922)
6349	bogie Composite (SR to LBSC design, 1924)
6369	Saloon Composite (LCD, 1887)
6375	bogie Saloon Composite (SEC, 1911)
46924	PLA (LBSC Cattle Wagon, 1922) owned by National Railway Museum

WAGONS

(in date of build order; pre-1948 vehicles shown with SR Island or Esso fleet numbers, post-1948 vehicles shown with BR or LT fleet numbers)

429S	5t Crane, 6-wheel (MR, ca. 1865; later IWC)
429SM	Crane Match (LSW, ca. 1890; later IWC)
?	Bembridge Wharf Crane (IWR, ?)
56046	10t Road Van (LSW, 1898)
62888	10t Dropside (Price & Reeves, 1899; later SEC)
59038, 59049, 59050	10t Bolster (LBSC, 1909, 1910 & 1910 resp.)
1231, 1343	13t Oil Tank (Royal Daylight/Esso, 1916 & 1918 resp.)
60579	10t Road Vehicle Truck (SR to LBSC design, 1923)
61056	20t Lowmac (SR to SEC design, 1923)
27744, 27766, 28345	10t Dropside (SR to LBSC design, 1924, 1924 & 1925 resp.)
27834	10t Coal (SR to LBSC design, 1925)
27910	13t Coal (SR, 1927)
55710	15t Goods Brake Van (SR, 1934)
483700, 483701, 483733, 483725	13t Dropside Ballast (BR, 1949)
450157, 450665, 451289, 451341, 451924, 452018, 452715, 453374	13t Bolster (BR, 1950-1959)
HW435, HW437	20t Ballast Hopper (LT, 1965)

EXTENSION TO WOOTTON

111. As the cutting seen in pictures 30 and 97 had been infilled, a new site for the station was necessary, east of the road. Much work was required to eliminate the 1 in 70 gradient here. The track is being laid on a white clay-impervious matting. (I.Whitlam)

112. Another eastward view, this time including the finished loop and platform. The former came into use on 21st August 1977 but the latter was delayed until 7 August 1986. Creeping clay banks had caused problems for the platform builders. The official opening was 31st May 1987. (S.Futcher)

113. Now we look west and see the same chapel roof recorded in picture 30 nearly 40 years earlier. The signal box is the one we met in picture 55 at Freshwater. Almost out of view is a van body in use as a waiting shelter. (S.Futcher)

114. *Invincible* runs round its train and exposes the water filler pipe and the ticket office. The latter was moved onto the platform during the Winter of 1995-96 to meet revised safety requirements regarding buffer stops and adjacent buildings. (M.Turvey)

115. Much of the trackbed was still in sound condition and so, after clearance, a road laying machine was hired to spread the new ballast evenly. Behind is a small roller compacting the material.. (R.MacDonald)

←———————— 116. The track had previously formed one line between Farnham and Alton and the down line between Brading and Sandown. It was laid by large working parties over many week-ends between Autumn 1989 and Easter 1991. This photograph shows the track approaching Ashey at Easter 1990. (R.MacDonald)

←———————— 117. The ballast was stored and distributed from Ashey. The platform here was not reopened until 2nd May 1993; it is visible in the background of this 1994 picture. (T.Heavyside)

118. No. 8 *Freshwater* runs towards Smallbrook Junction on 29th August 1994. A new boiler was built for this engine in 1997 at the same time as one for another "Terrier" (*Bodiam* at Rolvenden), probably the first example of quantity production in standard gauge preservation. (P.G.Barnes)

119. The bunting is out on the first day of public services, 21st July 1991. The nearest coach is no. 4112, seen under repair in picture 107; it is coupled to ex-IWR no. 46 - railway preservation at its best! (S.Futcher)

120. "All change", the staff announce on the platform on the right on 22nd July 1991, twenty years after the preservationists' final train had departed from Newport. Much had changed, but much had been successfully conserved for posterity. (M.Turvey)

MP Middleton Press

Easebourne Lane, Midhurst, West Sussex. GU29 9AZ Tel: 01730 813169 Fax: 01730 812601
. . . WRITE OR PHONE FOR OUR LATEST LIST . . .

BRANCH LINES
Branch Line to Allhallows
Branch Lines to Alton
Branch Lines around Ascot
Branch Line to Ashburton
Branch Lines around Bodmin
Branch Line to Bude
Branch Lines around Canterbury
Branch Line to Cheddar
Branch Lines to East Grinstead
Branch Lines to Effingham Junction
Branch Line to Fairford
Branch Line to Hawkhurst
Branch Line to Hayling
Branch Lines to Horsham
Branch Line to Ilfracombe
Branch Lines to Longmoor
Branch Line to Lyme Regis
Branch Line to Lynton
Branch Lines around Midhurst
Branch Line to Minehead
Branch Lines to Newport (IOW)
Branch Line to Padstow
Branch Lines around Plymouth
Branch Lines around Portmadoc 1923-46
Branch Lines around Porthmadog 1954-94
Branch Lines to Seaton & Sidmouth
Branch Line to Selsey
Branch Lines around Sheerness
Branch Line to Southwold
Branch Line to Swanage
Branch Line to Tenterden
Branch Lines to Torrington
Branch Lines to Tunbridge Wells
Branch Line to Upwell
Branch Lines around Wimborne
Branch Lines around Wisbech

SOUTH COAST RAILWAYS
Ashford to Dover
Brighton to Eastbourne
Chichester to Portsmouth
Dover to Ramsgate
Portsmouth to Southampton
Ryde to Ventnor
Worthing to Chichester

SOUTHERN MAIN LINES
Bromley South to Rochester
Charing Cross to Orpington
Crawley to Littlehampton
Dartford to Sittingbourne
East Croydon to Three Bridges
Epsom to Horsham
Exeter to Barnstaple
Exeter to Tavistock
Faversham to Dover
Haywards Heath to Seaford
London Bridge to East Croydon
Orpington to Tonbridge
Swanley to Ashford
Tavistock to Plymouth
Victoria to East Croydon
Waterloo to Woking
Waterloo to Windsor

Woking to Portsmouth
Woking to Southampton
Yeovil to Exeter

COUNTRY RAILWAY ROUTES
Andover to Southampton
Bournemouth to Evercreech Jn.
Burnham to Evercreech Junction
Croydon to East Grinstead
Fareham to Salisbury
Frome to Bristol
Guildford to Redhill
Porthmadog to Blaenau
Reading to Basingstoke
Reading to Guildford
Redhill to Ashford
Salisbury to Westbury
Strood to Paddock Wood
Taunton to Barnstaple
Wenford Bridge to Fowey
Westbury to Bath
Woking to Alton
Yeovil to Dorchester

GREAT RAILWAY ERAS
Ashford from Steam to Eurostar
Clapham Junction 50years of change
Festiniog in the Fifties
Festiniog in the Sixties
Isle of Wight Lines 50 years of change

LONDON SUBURBAN RAILWAYS
Caterham and Tattenham Corner
Clapham Jn. to Beckenham Jn.
Crystal Palace and Catford Loop
East London Line
Finsbury Park to Alexandra Palace
Holborn Viaduct to Lewisham
Lines around Wimbledon
London Bridge to Addiscombe
Mitcham Junction Lines
North London Line
South London Line
West Croydon to Epsom
West London Line
Willesden Junction to Richmond
Wimbledon to Epsom

STEAM PHOTOGRAPHERS
O.J.Morris's Southern Railways 1919-59

STEAMING THROUGH
Steaming through Cornwall
Steaming through East Sussex
Steaming through the Isle of Wight
Steaming through Kent
Steaming through West Hants
Steaming through West Sussex

TRAMWAY CLASSICS
Aldgate & Stepney Tramways
Barnet & Finchley Tramways
Bath Tramways
Bournemouth & Poole Tramways
Brighton's Tramways

Bristol's Tramways
Camberwell & W.Norwood Tramways
Croydon's Tramways
Clapham & Streatham Tramways
Dover's Tramways
East Ham & West Ham Tramways
Eltham & Woolwich Tramways
Embankment & Waterloo Tramways
Enfield & Wood Green Tramways
Exeter & Taunton Tramways
Gosport & Horndean Tramways
Greenwich & Dartford Tramways
Hampstead & Highgate Tramways
Hastings Tramways
Holborn & Finsbury Tramways
Ilford & Barking Tramways
Kingston & Wimbledon Tramways
Lewisham & Catford Tramways
Liverpool Tramways 1. Eastern Route
Maidstone & Chatham Tramways
North Kent Tramways
Portsmouth's Tramways
Reading Tramways
Seaton & Eastbourne Tramways
Southampton Tramways
Southend-on-sea Tramways
Southwark & Deptford Tramways
Stamford Hill Tramways
Thanet's Tramways
Victoria & Lambeth Tramways
Walthamstow & Leyton Tramways
Waltham Cross & Edmonton Tramway
Wandsworth & Battersea Tramways

TROLLEYBUS CLASSICS
Bournemouth Trolleybuses
Croydon's Trolleybuses
Maidstone Trolleybuses
Reading Trolleybuses
Woolwich & Dartford Trolleybuses

WATERWAY ALBUMS
Kent and East Sussex Waterways
London's Lost Route to the Sea
London to Portsmouth Waterway
Surrey Waterways

MILITARY BOOKS
Battle over Sussex 1940
Blitz over Sussex 1941-42
Bombers over Sussex 1943-45
Bognor at War
Military Defence of West Sussex
Secret Sussex Resistance

OTHER BOOKS
Betwixt Petersfield & Midhurst
Brickmaking in Sussex
Garraway Father & Son
Index to all Stations
London Chatham & Dover Railway
South Eastern & Chatham Railways

SOUTHERN RAILWAY VIDEO
War on the Line